Pebble® Plus

Animal Homes

Squirrels and Their Nests

by Martha E. H. Rustad

Consulting Editor: Gail Saunders-Smith, PhD

Consultant: William John Ripple, Professor
Oregon State University
Corvallis, Oregon

Capstone press®

Mankato, Minnesota

Pebble Plus is published by Capstone Press,
151 Good Counsel Drive, P.O. Box 669, Mankato, Minnesota 56002.
www.capstonepress.com

1 2 3 4 5 6 09 08 07 06 05 04

Library of Congress Cataloging-in-Publication Data
Rustad, Martha E. H. (Martha Elizabeth Hillman), 1975–
    Squirrels and their nests / by Martha E. H. Rustad.
    p. cm.—(Pebble plus. Animal homes)
    Includes bibliographical references (p. 23) and index.
    ISBN-13: 978-0-7368-2585-6 (hardcover)
    ISBN-10: 0-7368-2585-1 (hardcover)
    ISBN-13: 978-0-7368-5129-9 (softcover pbk.)
    ISBN-10: 0-7368-5129-1 (softcover pbk.)
    1. Squirrels—Nests—Juvenile literature. [1. Squirrels—Nests.]
I. Title. II. Animal homes (Mankato, Minn.)
QL737.R68 R85 2005
599.36—dc22   2003024905

Summary: Simple text and photographs illustrate squirrels and their nests.

Editorial Credits
Mari C. Schuh, editor; Linda Clavel, series designer; Enoch Peterson, book designer;
    Kelly Garvin, photo researcher; Karen Hieb, product planning editor

Photo Credits
Ann & Rob Simpson, 11
Bruce Coleman Inc./E. R. Degginger, 8–9; Erwin & Peggy Bauer, 17; Hans Reinhard, 15; John E. Swedberg, 21
Corbis/Ian Beames, 19
Dwight R. Kuhn, 5
James M. Mejuto, 6–7
Minden Pictures/Michael Quinton, cover
PhotoDisc Inc., 1
Tom & Pat Leeson, 12–13

Note to Parents and Teachers

The Animal Homes series supports national science standards related to life science. This book describes and illustrates squirrels and their nests. The images support early readers in understanding the text. The repetition of words and phrases helps early readers learn new words. This book also introduces early readers to subject-specific vocabulary words, which are defined in the Glossary section. Early readers may need assistance to read some words and to use the Table of Contents, Glossary, Read More, Internet Sites, and Index/Word List sections of the book.

Word Count: 130
Early-Intervention Level: 15

Table of Contents

Building a Home

Squirrels are small rodents that live in trees. Squirrels build stick nests and dens.

Stick Nests

Squirrels build stick nests
in trees. They use leaves
and sticks for the nests.

Squirrels put leaves, fur,
and moss inside stick nests.

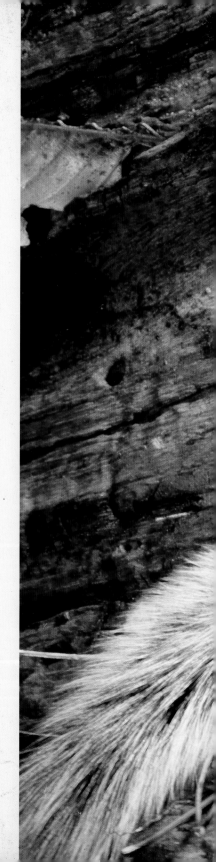

Dens

Squirrels build dens in hollow trees. Squirrels also live in tree holes made by other animals.

Squirrels line dens with grass, moss, and leaves. Squirrels sometimes take days to build their homes.

Squirrels store food in
their homes. Squirrels
eat nuts and seeds.

Young Squirrels

Young squirrels are born
in stick nests or dens.
Two to eight young squirrels
are born at a time.

Young squirrels stay safe and warm in their homes. Female squirrels take care of them.

A Good Home

Squirrels sometimes live in
both stick nests and dens.
These places are good
homes for squirrels.

Glossary

den—a squirrel nest in a hollow space in a tree

hollow—to have an empty space inside

moss—a soft plant with no roots

rodent—a mammal with large, sharp front teeth; squirrels, rats, beavers, and prairie dogs are rodents.

safe—not in danger of being hurt

stick nest—a home and shelter built by squirrels in tree branches

Read More

Schaefer, Lola M. *Squirrels.* My Big Backyard. Chicago: Heinemann Library, 2004.

Swanson, Diane. *Squirrels.* Welcome to the World of Animals. Milwaukee: Gareth Stevens, 2003.

Townsend, Emily Rose. *Squirrels.* Woodland Animals. Mankato, Minn.: Pebble Books, 2004.

Internet Sites

FactHound offers a safe, fun way to find Internet sites related to this book. All of the sites on FactHound have been researched by our staff.

Here's how:

1. Visit *www.facthound.com*

2. Type in this special code **0736825851** for age-appropriate sites. Or enter a search word related to this book for a more general search.

3. Click on the **Fetch It** button.

FactHound will fetch the best sites for you!

Index/Word List